The Selling Mindset Series

HOW TO BOOST YOUR SALES VALUE

DAPO ONAMUSI

©2020 by Dapo Onamusi

Be advised strictly that scanning, uploading, and electronic sharing of any part of this book without the permission of the publisher is unlawful piracy and theft of the author's intellectual property. Such acts would be prosecuted by law.

If you would like to use material from this book (other than for review purposes), prior written permission must be obtained by contacting the publisher at dafixcompany@gmail.com

Thank you for your support of the author's rights.

DAFIX COMPANY
www.dafixcompany.com

Cover design by Dafix Company

First Edition: January 2020

The author and publisher do not lay any claim whatsoever to credit for the images used in this book, as they were sourced from public domain and used only for illustrative purposes.

THERE ARE SEVEN BOOKS IN THE SELLING MINDSET SERIES

HOW TO BOOST YOUR SALES VALUE

THE SELLING ENERGY

ANYBODY CAN SELL. EVEN YOU!

THE ART OF GIVE AND TAKE

BUSINESS IQ VERSUS EQ

THE ATTITUDE CUSTOMERS LOVE

ACTIVATE THE 3Cs OF SELLING

DISCLAIMER

Although the author and publisher have made every effort to ensure that the information in this book was correct at press time, the author and publisher do not assume and hereby disclaim any liability to any party for any loss, damage, or disruption caused by errors or omissions result from negligence, accident, or any other cause.

The information in this book is general advice only. It has been prepared without fully taking into account the reader's sales objectives, financial situation or business needs. Before acting on this advice the reader should consider the appropriateness of the advice, having regard to his/her own sales objectives, financial situation and business needs.

The author and publisher hereby disclaim all responsibility and liability to any person, arising directly or indirectly from any person taking or not taking action based on the information in this book.

DEDICATION

This book is dedicated to every business owner, business employee and value provider out there, looking for the road to their respective markets. I hope you find your paths early.

ACKNOWLEDGEMENTS

I acknowledge you, my #1 AC, for believing in me for two decades now, building a happy home with me and helping me manage these gifts. Thanks Tina for being my memory card and of course, the proud editor of this book.

I acknowledge you all, my maps and mirrors, for shining the light on my path when the times are dark, for sharing your wisdom and resources when I'm at my wits end. Allow me not to mention your names here. You know yourselves.

I acknowledge you ABBA. You're the real MVP!

FOREWORD

This is an extremely powerful contribution from Dapo Onamusi, with practical tips obviously gathered from days on the streets.

I have sat under his teachings many times, and come out the better each time. So it's really nice to see him finally document some of his wise nuggets in a book.

Even more exciting for me is his ability to communicate invaluable principles and knowledge using easy to digest words and colorful images to teach.

This book, has implications far beyond the obvious presentation, because selling really is the most important skill anyone can and should possess. Everyone of us is either selling, or being sold to every waking moment.

This is Dapo's first commercially published book, but he has complete control of his craft and his style. Thankfully it's a series. I strongly recommend that you read the book all through, and watch it.

You are about to "blow" your sales target.
Enjoy!

Olusoji Oyawoye
Coach, Mentor and Social Entrepreneur
Certified Coach of The John Maxwell Team

TABLE OF CONTENTS

INTRODUCTION	x
PART ONE	1
THINGS YOU NEED TO KNOW	2
CHAPTER 1	3
Do You Really Understand Value?	3
CHAPTER 2	17
See Why Customers Love Value	17
CHAPTER 3	33
The Science Of Value	33

PART TWO	49
THINGS YOU NEED TO DO	50
CHAPTER 4	51
Use Value To Boost Your Sales	51
CHAPTER 5	61
How To Sell At Your Own Price	61
CONCLUSION	87
READER'S REVIEW	90
GET IN TOUCH	91
ABOUT THE AUTHOR	92
OTHER BOOKS IN THE SERIES	93

INTRODUCTION

'How to Boost Your Sales Value' is one of the 7 killer bundles in 'The Selling Mindset Series' authored by design thinker and business consultant, Dapo Onamusi. This series is compiled, in response to a deep yearning from Startups and Medium Scale Business Owners that are struggling with closing the wide gap between their business offerings and customer engagement and patronage.

As a Sales and Marketing Coach, having trained several business owners and employees in key sales and marketing related functions, Dapo understands their concerns and has outlined in this series, a number of easy-to-understand, technical jargon-free things they could do differently to realize their business conversion targets.

For over 20 years, Dapo Onamusi has worked actively in different areas of Marketing Communications - Brands Design & Management, Advertising, Strategy, Creative, Media, Production etc and has helped different businesses, home and abroad achieve their marketing objectives and deliver on their bottom line.

In the course of his career, Dapo has tried a number of ideas that failed, he has also tried quite a number of ideas that hit significant successes. In all of these, he has learnt what works and what doesn't, most of which he shares in his trainings and unpublished writings.

To get the best out of *The Selling Mindset* and answer the question *"Can I Buy from Myself?"*, it is recommended that you get all the killer bundles in the series.

PART ONE

THINGS YOU NEED TO KNOW

CHAPTER 1

DO YOU REALLY UNDERSTAND VALUE?

"Value is what an individual perceives he or she desires in a person, place or thing."

As we open up the subject of boosting sales value in our businesses, we will focus on 3 key elements - *value*, the *value provider* and the *customer*. Now notice that there are two basic definitions of value - one refers to the worth of something, while the other refers to standards of behavior. Examples of the latter definition are those attributes people adopt as their way of life, or the ones you see in company profiles that form acronyms out of positive traits, but in this book, we will focus on the former definition: the worth of something.

Pay close attention to what will be shared in this bundle. At the end of this piece, you will fully understand and grasp how you can leverage on VALUE to your best advantage and generate more sales volumes. In different parts of this book, I'll be referring to you the reader either as a business owner or a value provider. Even if you are not a business owner, or you are an employee, or a regular Joe who is interested in this book, I am referring to you all the same.

As a business owner, you definitely have an understanding of value, but this book seeks to dig a little deeper beyond what the regular eyes can see. To explore the concept of value, you need more than your regular eyes. You need all your senses. This is where PERCEPTION comes in. I'd refer to 'perception' as the glasses you need to put on so you can see beyond the regular eyes and fully understand Value and how it works. Value is incomplete, if it is not fully perceived.

Perception goes beyond sight, it is what your senses inform your mind about a thing or a concept. Perception doesn't necessarily need to be factual or accurate, as long as it is translated to the mind; that is the reality that the mind adopts and acts upon. Every decision and action that man makes or takes are based on the information his mind perceives, it doesn't matter whether the source is accurate or not.

For instance, the late Nigerian musician, Fela Anikulapo Kuti would be perceived by some as troublesome, while to others as a legend.

The colour Turquoise would be perceived by some as blue, while to others as green (I even heard of an option called teal).

Tomatoes all over the world till today are debated and perceived both as fruit and vegetable.

I can as well throw this out there - Who do you perceive is the world's greatest soccer player between Messi and Ronaldo? *(You get the idea).*

Therefore, value doesn't need to be accurate, or generally acceptable, it only needs to be interpreted the way the individual perceives it. So what is value?

Value (with regards to the worth of something) is a combination of different expressions - Attributes, Benefits, Importance, Relevance, Usefulness, Worth, Estimate, Appreciation, Quality, the list goes on.

Simply put, allow me to define Value as follows:

"Value is what an individual (vendor or customer) perceives he or she desires in a person, place or thing."

You'd notice two keywords used in my definition above - *perceive* and *desire*. All the different expressions of value I listed above are often the expressions 'desired' by the individual, thus the mind is wired to seek and identify these expressions. So whenever the mind 'perceives' any of these expressions, the individual is attracted to such desires, to the point of giving whatever he or she has (cash or kind) in exchange for such value. That is how buying and selling is done.

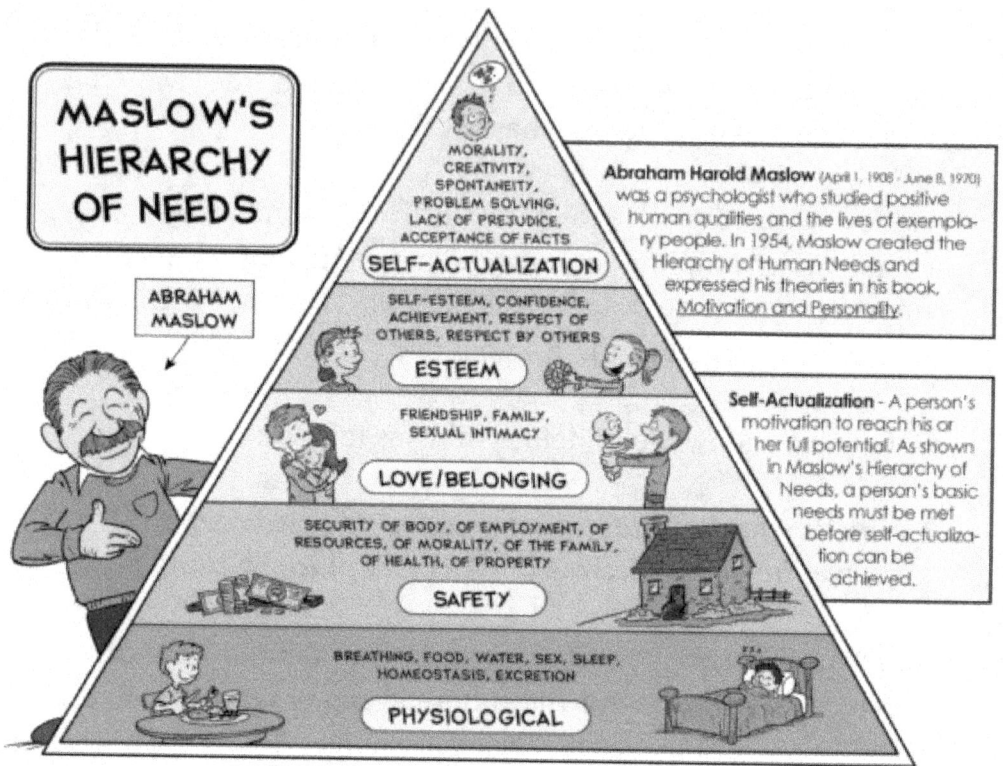

As a business owner or employee, you understand that your business is set up to anticipate, identify and satisfy your customers' needs, right? That is Marketing in a nutshell. If you look at Marslow's analysis of the hierarchy of needs, you'll understand that everything stacked up in the pyramid is in one way or another an expression of value (refer to the illustration above).

Whether your customer's needs are *physiological, safety, love or belonging, esteem or self-actualization,* depending on the individual's level of need, his or her desire would be different and his or her scope or value perception would definitely be different as well.

Another thing you must understand is that the same value in a person, place or thing can be perceived differently and thus, create different desires for different individuals. If we use 'a woman' for example, different individuals would perceive they desire different things in her:
- A man would desire a girlfriend or a wife in her
- A fellow woman would desire a friend or confidant in her
- A child would desire a mother or a guardian in the same woman

The list goes on, but you can see that the same woman is perceived as different things to different people.

Having this knowledge at the back of your mind, you need to take a second look at what you're offering your customers. You may have assumed you know what desire they perceived in your offering, but your assumptions could be limited or in some cases, misplaced.

Take a thorough assessment of your value offering, what it means to you and what it means to your customers. You also need to understand that the same value you offer may mean different things to different customers.

For instance, if you're an artist selling art pieces, what your value offering means to a bank (that has numerous branches in its network) will definitely be different from a hotel (that has a number of rooms). Same value will be perceived differently by an art collector who runs a museum and received differently by an individual who just wants the pieces in his home for the sheer love of art.

In any of these cases, you will have to consider a number of factors to assign value to your work. Factors like exclusivity of the art pieces (for clients who want exclusivity) and reproduction of copies (for clients who don't mind). Another factor to consider would be the level of passion these customers have for art (very important, as this would determine how much they would appreciate your work). Last, but definitely not the least is how renowned you are as an artist.

This analysis applies to you as well, even if you're not an artist. You can take a survey of the types of customers you serve, regardless of your line of business. Understand their quantity and quality.

Take a careful study of Marslow's chart above and determine which of the 5 levels of need your value is designed to meet:
1. Physiological
2. Safety
3. Love or Belonging
4. Esteem
5. Self-actualization

Note that the higher the level of need as you climb the pyramid, the fewer your customers would be and the more value you assign to your offering. On the flip side, the lower the level of need as you descend the pyramid, the larger your customer numbers and the less value you assign to your offering. Also consider the factors that will help you assign value to your offering, using the examples given for the artist above as a guide.

A very good example of this value offering is the most expensive book ever sold. It can be argued that this book met a Self-actualization need, as it was definitely not targeted at a large number of customers at all.

Sold at Christie's auction house in New York to Bill Gates in November 1994, at a whooping final price of $30.8 million (about $53 million / €50 million today at inflation adjusted price), Codex Leicester stands as the most expensive book ever sold.

Codex Leicester, also referred to as the Codex Hammer, was hand-written by Leonardo da Vinci in 1510. The 72-page linen journal featured the author's point of view on different scientific theories like why the moon is luminous, movement of water and how to find fossils.

Bill Gates, being a wealthy customer couldn't have been a more appropriate buyer of the book, which has been passed down from different previous owners over generations - Giuseppe Ghezzi, Thomas Coke and Armand Hammer.

Bill Gates loved science, appreciated the value of the book and more importantly, could afford to buy the book!

Let's take another look at Marslow's 5 levels of need. Did you know that within each of the 5 levels of need you meet, you can further classify the value you offer? For instance, if your business is designed to meet a physiological need like food, you can further determine the value of your food business.

Let's take a look at the difference between a Fine Dining Restaurant and a Quick Service Restaurant (QSR). Despite the fact that they both meet physiological needs, their values are classified differently. The Fine Dining Restaurant serves fewer customer numbers with higher value offering, while the Quick Service Restaurant serves larger customer numbers with lower value offering.

For the Fine Dining Restaurant, there is a chef on ground, available to 'freshly prepare' the customer's order from the special menu of cuisines provided. While the customer waits for his order, he is occupied with some form of entertainment and classy customer experience by the waiters on stand by. The order is served in an elegant fashion at the customer's table, based on the number of courses. After a wonderful dining experience, the customer is presented with a bill which is settled (in some cases with a tip, to appreciate the service provided).

For the Quick Service Restaurant however, the meals are prepared ahead of time before the customers visit. Customers order from a menu of ready-to-eat meals available and make payment. The meals are served almost immediately to the customers across the counter. Depending on the layout of the QSR, customers may eat-in or take-out their meals. For eat-in customers, they may be provided with some form of entertainment and customer experience as added value.

As a value provider, it is your call to determine the kind of value you want to offer your customers, knowing that whatever type of value you offer would determine how much customers you would attract and how much they would be willing to pay for your offering.

CHAPTER 2

SEE WHY CUSTOMERS LOVE VALUE

"Understand the specific reason why customers buy"

In one of my training sessions (SELL MORE THRU THE BACK DOOR 2.0), I asked the participants some key questions:
- What was the last thing your customer bought from you?
- Why did they buy it?
- Why from you?

I strongly recommend that you ask yourselves these questions everyday. In fact, if you have a vision board or a notice board in your office or business outlet, write out these questions boldly and post it there. Share with your team as well. This will help you figure out why your customers buy and help you position your offering as always spot on in meeting your customers' desire.

For instance, if your customer buys a red box from you, don't just be happy that the till rings. Find out if your customer bought a piece of storage, a footstool or a photography prop. For all you care, it might be a stepping block for heights or a gift item. That will help you understand your customer better and position your business offerings properly to satisfy his/her desires, both present and future.

Now let's talk about Desire. In the previous chapter, we touched briefly on this, so let's go a little deeper. This is one of the best kept secret in Sales. If you didn't know before now, note this. In fact, get a marker and highlight this, tweet it to my credit, post it or make it your wallpaper.

"Desire is one of the best kept secret in Sales".

Whether you're into products or services, what you're selling may be a commodity, but what your customer is buying is a desire.

Take a look at the following business offerings and see them from your customers' point of view:

You sell Wedding Gowns (but the customer buys a desire to be the most talked about person at the wedding or a feature or center of attraction at Vanity Fair or Bellanaija)

You sell Plane Tickets (but the customer buys a desire for an amazing trip, a status symbol, a seat next to someone important)

You sell Body Shapers (but the customer buys a desire to 'slay' in those photographs, feel good and look slim, curvy and attractive to guys in those dresses)

You sell Human hair wigs (but the customer buys a desire to be beautiful, without the need for multiple salon visits)

You sell the latest Gadgets or Devices (but the customer buys a desire for social validation, to brag about his/her trendsetting status to everyone that cares to know)

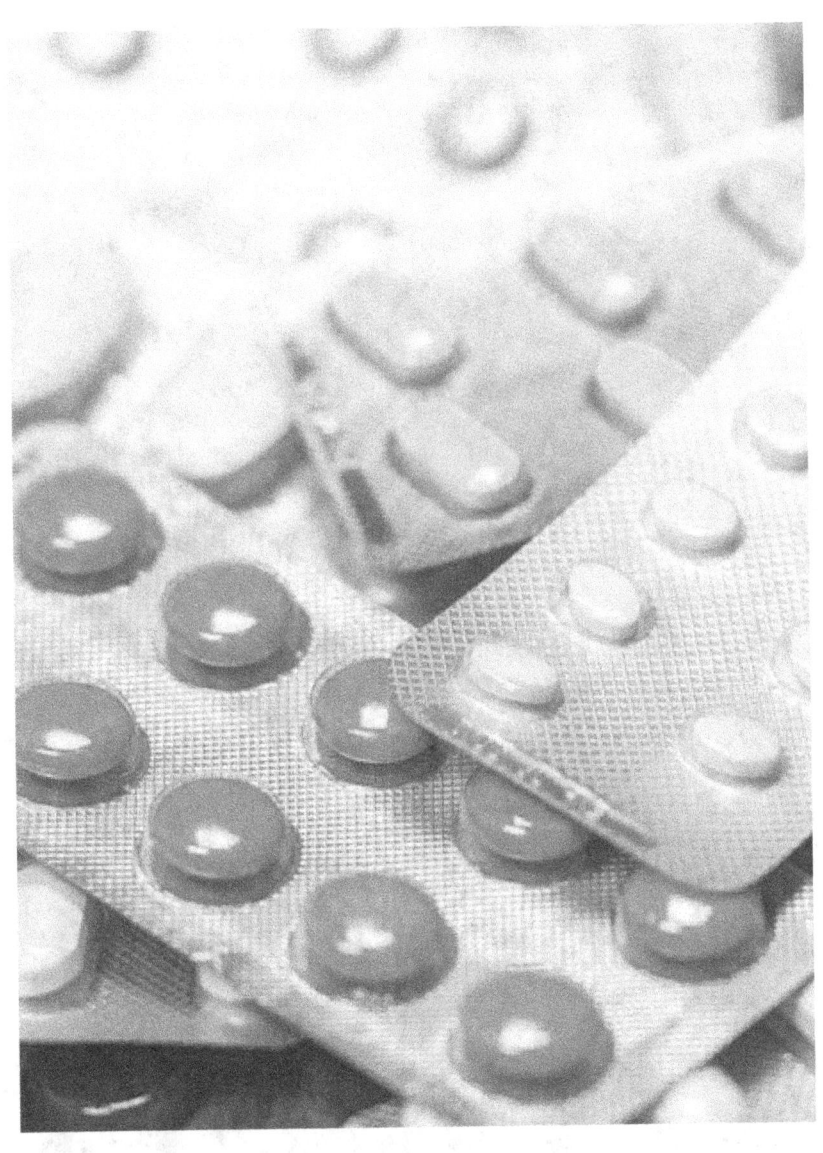

You sell Medications (but the customer buys a desire to be in optimal health or enjoy well being at its fullest without much downtime or unproductive bed ridden moments)

You sell Landed Property (but the customer buys a desire to validate his/her self worth or net worth or self confidence, a worthy investment or an association with desirable neighbours)

You sell Developed Houses (but the customer buys a desire to relax after a busy day, or invite guests over and impress them, or make a statement of class in his/her neighborhood)

You sell cars like the Toyota Corolla (but the customer buys a desire to move about conveniently with low maintenance costs)

You sell cars like the Lexus LX570 (but the customer buys a desire to step out of the middle class)

You sell cars like the Aston Martin db11 (but the customer buys a desire to make a royal statement)

*In comparison, one db11 = three LX570s = twelve Corollas

Now the desires I've interpreted here are not exhaustive as the desires perceived by the customer. Never assume that you know what desire exactly you're satisfying with your products or services until you have conducted extensive investigations. This will help you sharpen your value propositions to your customers and increase your probability of successful sales.

A Smartphone for instance, could be a personal assistant to a busy executive, a camera to a professional photographer, a memo pad or I-witness widget to a journalist, a content creator to a blogger, a cooking documentary maker to a chef, a mobile studio to a recording artist. The list is endless. Take a second look at who your customer really is and the value your product or service is providing for them.

As you can see, understanding the concept of value is not a straight forward, easy, one-size-fits-all process. You need to tailor it specifically to your business and to your target market. Only then can you engage your customer in your favour at the negotiation table over discussions of price points for the value you offer.

Let me conclude this chapter with a story I heard somewhere. A father, before he died, said to his son: "This is the watch your grandfather gave me and this is more than 200 years old. Before I give it to you, go to the watch shop on the first street, tell the watchmaker I want to sell it, and ask how much he'll offer".

The son went and after several minutes, he came back to his father and said, "The watchmaker offers to pay $50 because it's old and has a lot of scratches." He then asked the son to go to the coffee shop. The son went and after an hour came back shocked and disappointed. He said: "The coffee shop owner offers $5, father."

"Go to the museum and show them the watch" the father said again. He went ahead and then came back happily. He said "They offered me a million dollars for this piece."

The father said: *"I wanted you to know the right place where you are valued, don't put yourself in the wrong place and get angry if you get treated like trash. Those who know your value are the ones who appreciate you, don't ever stay in a place that doesn't suit you."*

The lesson is simple. You are not sent to be everything to everyone. Not everyone is meant to be your customer. Separate the prospects from the suspects. Find and focus on your customer who appreciates the value of what you offer.

A Junkie needs a Fix.
A Junkie appreciates the value of a Fix.
A Junkie never turns his back on a Fix.
A Junkie finds the means for a Fix.
Be the Fix. Make your customer a Junkie
Because a Junkie will always come back for a Fix. ©

CHAPTER 3

THE SCIENCE OF VALUE

"Explore the different factors that affect how value is perceived by the end user"

When you fully grasp the value you're offering your customers, only then can you command a price of your choice in exchange for your value. Before you can fully grasp the value you're offering your customers, you need to understand the Science of Value.

Yes, there is a Science to Value - a Biology, Chemistry and Physics of Value. Value has life. It grows, moves, breathes, appreciates, depreciates, reproduces, responds to senses and value also dies. Value can be combined for good or ill. Value can be transmitted from one medium to another by association. Value can also be relative, meaning different things to different people.

The Science of Value seeks to explore the different factors that affect how value is perceived by the end user. Some of these factors include personal preference, time, circumstance, location, market forces and policies.

PERSONAL PREFERENCE

Let's take a lady who is more passionate about bags and less about gadgets. She will easily justify the benefits of a $4000 Louis Vuitton Twist MM 3D Damier Bag and in the same

breath, consider it ridiculous that a home computer like the 27-inch Apple iMac would cost as much as $2000.

That is some insight, right there. To sell effectively, you need to do your homework in finding your ideal customer, who understands and appreciates the value of what you are selling.

The Fall/Winter 2019 edition of the *Louis Vuitton Twist MM 3D Damier Bag* will definitely appeal to someone who has a copy of the previous edition of the bag, or a similar product within that class.

Such a person understands and appreciates the value of the product already, so you don't need much convincing. In fact, there is a good possibility that such customer is in the market for a trade off or an upgrade.

This method is useful for targeting your market effectively, as you look out for insights in customer profiles, interests and behaviors.

If you go back in time, before money was invented, trade by barter was basically exchange of values, as perceived by the trading parties. In some cases, you'd see a poultry farmer trading a crate of eggs in exchange for a jerrycan of palm wine. In today's world, both commodities may not be worth the same, but to the trading parties what they wanted in exchange was satisfactory in value to them. That is personal preference value.

This is the same reason a family relocating out of country would dispose their home effects at knock off rates in exchange for traveling cash. For this category of people, it is easy to assume that all they want is just cash, right? Well, you'll never know who is interested in a viable investment instrument, for those who want to have something working for them as a guaranteed asset back in their home country while they're out of town. If you are into investment products, you might just be in luck if you creatively position your value to such people.

TIME

They say time is money, isn't it? What is the value of a political campaign after election? Medicine after death? Running after you missed your flight? That is the illustration of time value. The striking feature of time value is its lifespan, one minute it's of tremendous value, the next minute, it's useless.

We can look at time value from the scope of trends. Take for example, the average price of a wedding gown is $1000. We all know you can get a wedding gown for as low as $100, just as you can get one for as high as $100,000. Either-way, the emotional and rational value of the wedding gown is expressed, based on the disposable income available to the customer, right? Now imagine trying to sell the same wedding gown to a bride, the week after her wedding. What value would she place on it? Even if you give her for free, she might not even say 'thank you'.

In the previous chapter, recall that I talked about Bill Gates buying the most expensive book ever sold. Timing is very key here. He bought the book about a month after his 39th birthday. Even though he was not the richest man in the world yet, he was wealthy enough to make such audacious move.

At 39, he was playing active roles in the day-to-day affairs of Microsoft as CEO and work was underway for the release of the Windows 95 operating system. After Bill Gates bought the *Codex Leicester by Leonardo da Vinci*, he scanned many of the pages and used them as wallpapers and screensavers in the operating system, released the following year.

Fast forward to the time of writing this book, if you consider the present lifestyle of Bill Gates in his 60s, playing passive roles in Microsoft, taking up more interests in humanitarian activities and philanthropy, he might not be the most appropriate customer for the book if it was auctioned today. Of course, he can still afford it, however, it might not come up as top priority for him.

As a business person, you must understand and fully optimize the time value of your products and services in your business interest. For instance, a piping hot pizza, fresh out of the oven is a yummy delight, worth a great deal within minutes. After an hour, the same pizza left unattended is cold, dry and of less value. In fact, there are some pizza outlets that promise to deliver their pizzas piping hot, else the customer gets it free of charge.

We can also look at time value from the scope of seasons. For regions where food processing and preservation is not the norm, when a crop is in season, it is in abundance and the value is almost taken for granted. When it gets out of season, the price point shoots up in response to its scarcity, thus its value increases.

Umbrellas, raincoats/winter coats are better valued during the rainy/winter season. Anyone selling ice cold drinks in cold weather, will need a miracle to find customers, as you can imagine.

In Nigeria, West Africa, the weather sometimes could be in extreme temperatures. When it's hot, you could almost fry an omelette right under the sun without a stove; on the flip side, when it's cold, people would react with a flu.

If you're living in Lagos and you're used to life on the streets, you'd notice trolley pushers from a major coffee brand that sells hot ready-to-drink coffee at bus stops and busy streets when the whether is cool, right? When the weather becomes hot, the coffee disappears while the major bus stops and traffic stops will be littered with ice cold soda pops!

Major soda brands within the West African region understand the impact of the seasonal trend on their businesses very well. As consumption of their products soars during the dry season, their production capacity is ramped up accordingly to meet the demand. When the rainy season kicks in, they support the consumption drop with all kinds of promotional activities and support collaterals for their distribution channels to boost sales.

Another scope of time value is urgency. For example, if you book a flight, 30 days ahead of time, the value of the plane ticket will definitely be different from the value if you book your flight the night before (same trip, same plane, same fuel, same distance, same cabin crew service). That means everybody on board the same flight cabin, paid different prices for their seats, depending on when they booked.

In the health sector, the value of treatment for a condition that is not terminal is nothing compared to the value of treatment of a chronic, terminal condition. Have you wondered why the cost of chemotherapy, radiology and dialysis are way higher than costs of ultrasound, X-rays and even fracture P.O.P. casts?

One more scope of time value is age. Some items appreciate with age, while some depreciate with age. A brand new car depreciates as much as 11% of its value once it leaves the showroom, and can lose up to 30% in the first year. In Real Estate, there's a bit of an irony, as a built up property tends to depreciate over time, while the land it sits on typically appreciates in value (thanks to the increasing population versus constant land mass).

CIRCUMSTANCE

Imagine that you've been out all day and you get back to the comfort of your home, really thirsty and dehydrated. Your throat is parched and you know what exactly you're longing for to quench that thirst real fast. Now how would you react if you were told that there's no water or drink available at home, not even a drop?

To make things more interesting, what if you were presented instead, with a sumptuous spread of your favorite food - pasta? How would you deal with the mixed feelings? As much as your favorite food is quite valuable, you'd agree with me that you'd rather trade all that spread for a refreshing glass of cool drink at that point in time.

Let's take it up a notch. Imagine trying to foot the healthcare bill for an emergency situation without any health insurance cover. In that situation, the only thing on your mind is survival. You'd go to any length, by all means possible to get access to that emergency healthcare.

Even if you run out of personal resources, you'll definitely explore options outside your means, beg, borrow or steal if necessary. The value of the treatment to you at that point of need is significantly higher, compared to when there is no emergency or urgency.

LOCATION

The usual suspect is Real Estate, right? Have you ever considered how a geographical location ends up being high brow, sub-urban or rural? It's the people! Whenever a collective number of people decide to treat their environment according to their personality, the result is always reflected on the value placed on the neighborhood eventually.

Take a look at a place previously known as Maroko, a low income community in Victoria Island, Lagos, Nigeria back in the 80s. It was a reflection of its 300,000 inhabitants. The moment the residents were swapped with a different crop of people, the location appreciated, playing host to facilities like Four Points by Sheraton, Palms Shopping Mall, Landmark Events Centre, Oriental Hotel and British International School.

Another approach to locational value is the influence of culture. Craft shops are common destinations all over the world, where locals sell hand made decorated pieces (fabrics, fashion accessories, art works etc.) that reflect their home lands. To foreign visitors, these pieces are valuable memorabilia of their visits to such places, while to the locals the items may mean next to nothing.

MARKET FORCES

Market forces represent the most common illustration of value in the business world. We learnt from elementary Economics about how the forces of demand and supply affect price. As a business owner, you can also optimize any of the forces in your business interest, to deliver value to your customer. For instance, whenever there is shortage in supply of Premium Motor Spirit (petrol) in Nigeria, vendors who can provide the commodity make the most of the business.

Another example is the beehive of activities in the market during festive periods. As the demand for festivity-related items (food, clothes, gifts etc) increase, discerning business people will position themselves, not to take the demand for granted, but to be the preferred supplier of the commodities to the customer. The more customers you can attract and provide with an irresistible and irreplaceable experience during this period, the more you're likely to retain when the festivity is over.

POLICIES

One of the powers conferred on our leaders in government is the ability to determine the value of commodities, through the policies they implement while in office. The first expression of this is foreign investment. We all know that a country's level of attraction to investors is subject to the attitude and body language of it's leaders. Foreign investment in a country affects prices of certain commodities, level of opportunities available and economic development through job creations, which also affect disposable income for the customer.

Another expression of policies is imports and exports. This creates mutual benefits for the trading countries, it also enables availability of products and services upon demand. A friendly import and export policy automatically translate to friendly evaluation of trading stock. Areas of concern include determination of acceptable or banned commodities in the interest of the country and appropriation of custom duties & other government levies. Where unfriendly import and export policies are in place, the hydra headed monster of scarcity of commodities, border tensions, smuggling and related crimes trouble the market.

For example, at the time of writing this book, an order had been placed by the Nigerian government without prior warning to close all her land borders and stop all imports and exports from and to her neighbouring countries through the land borders.

This order, according to the Nigerian government, was in response to a high influx of food items from neighbouring countries, which the Nigerian government perceived was threatening the growth of local production, especially rice from Benin Republic.

There had been series of events leading to these land borders closure. Many years ago, rice was initially a meal for the upper-middle class and was consumed on special occasions. Nigeria was producing most of its food items locally, including rice, however the capacity of its output was far from meeting the demands of its growing population of over 200 million.

To meet this shortfall, importation of rice was allowed through her sea ports, with a stiff duty of 70%. This was planned to generate revenue, while encouraging local production.

However, there was a twist to the tale. Smugglers had found a much cheaper route - the Benin corridor next door, that had crashed its tax to an attractive 7%. In a short while, the Benin Republic became the conduit for importing rice into Nigeria, with a whooping 80% of her imports from Thailand eventually landing in Nigeria.

Over time, rice became a much more affordable staple for all classes of Nigerians as they can't seem to get enough of it, not to mention their growing fondness for the flagship recipe - Jollof Rice.

This booming smuggling business through the Benin border forced the Nigerian government to place a ban on importation of rice, but the ban was barely effective as the smugglers got more creative.

This rice abundance, smuggled in without control became a serious threat to local production that didn't stand a competitive chance. At the climax of events, the Nigerian government ordered the closure of her land borders without warning.

Following the series of events leading to the eventual closure of the land borders, there had been significant effect of government policies on the rise and fall of the price of rice over the years. Local production has increased over the years, but the country is still far from meeting her domestic demands. At the moment of writing this book, the price of rice (both locally produced and imported) was perceived to be on the high side.

One more expression of policies is Internal Finance. This is where arms of government like the apex bank of a country comes in. Regulation/valuation of currencies, banking laws, implementation of subsidies and taxes definitely affect perceived value of things.

For instance, the Central Bank of Nigeria (CBN) is enacted to ensure monetary and price stability, issue legal tender currency in the country and maintain external reserves to safeguard the international value of the local currency. The CBN is also responsible for administering the other banks and financial institutions in the country.

Recently (at the time of writing), the CBN issued a circular to its member banks and financial institutions, guiding them to a downward review of charges across a number of financial activities carried out by the end customers, individuals and businesses.

These reviewed charges affect a number of financial activities, including maintenance of customer bank cards, withdrawals from Automated Teller Machines (ATMs), electronic transfers, reactivation of savings accounts and maintenance of current accounts.

This move was well received by customers who erstwhile had to deal with higher charges in their banking transactions, thereby limiting their spending power.

According to the Law of Demand, this implies that before the CBN review of the charges, customers would struggle to purchase goods that are in supply due to their limited means. With the CBN lower charges in effect, customers would experience an increase in their spending power and demand will increase.

In summary, a conscious awareness of these factors are quite helpful for you as a business owner, to help you understand your product, your market, your political climate and everything else it takes to make your sales successful, year in, year out.

PART TWO

THINGS YOU NEED TO DO

CHAPTER 4

USE VALUE TO BOOST YOUR SALES

"Find out if and why your customers want it, then leverage on the desire your offering is satisfying"

Now that you are more enlightened about the concept of value, what are you going to do about this knowledge? If you're thinking what I'm thinking, then you're on track. You need to review your business offering and ask yourself honest questions like "Can I really buy from Myself?"

I watched an episode of 'Invent It Rich' - a TV show. The concept of the show is to have different inventor startups present their ideas before a Venture Capitalist who would invest in the most valuable idea.

In this episode, some tech guys invented a toy drone that you could control with your mind, sort of. A head set with sensors is worn on the head, which picks up focus signals from the brain and transforms the signals into electric switches to control the toy drone. The idea of controlling a toy drone with the mind was cool, no doubt, but the fancy was short lived.

While the idea scored average at the prototype testing stage, it dropped below average at the consumer appraisal stage. At the consumer appraisal stage, a room full of regular people were appointed as a jury-customers to appraise the different ideas from different contestants and decide if they liked the ideas and how much they would be willing to pay for such invented products.

When the consumers got to the toy drones stand, they had a bit of trouble understanding how the product worked. What's more, they wondered if they really needed the toy in their lives - ouch!

The inventors of the mind-controlled toy drones were really disappointed because they didn't make it to the investors table. They were even more disappointed that the market was not ready for their products. It was a piece of technology ahead of its time and the cost of such technology was way more than what the consumers were willing to pay for.

What did I learn from the show? User-friendliness and Relevance. Often times most business owners are super excited about their business offerings that they pay little or no attention to customer's desire or feedback. If you recall my definition of value (what an individual perceives he or she desires in a person, place or thing), then you would subject your business to the brutal test.

As a business person, it's okay to be happy about the positive feedbacks you get about your business, but it is more important that you take in graciously and focus more on the negative feedbacks. Appreciate and encourage the sincerity of the sources, investigate the processes that led to the negative feedbacks and firm up strategies to correct them or prevent a reoccurrence. By doing this, your customers not only feel regarded that you considered their feedback, they also enjoy a better business experience in the future.

What does your customer perceive he or she desires in your business? This is the question you must set out to answer everyday you open shop. Never look at your product or service with your regular eyes as a commodity anymore. Always try to perceive what your customer desires about it. Remember the three questions I gave you in chapter one? Put them to test everyday.

Whatever product or service you're delivering as a business, always find out extensively from your customers if and why they want it, then leverage on the desire it is satisfying.

This brings us to understanding the difference between rational value and emotional value. As much as rational value speaks to the technical specifications and functional attributes of a business offering, emotional value speaks to how buying into the offering makes the customer feel.

An example most men can relate to is cars. Let's talk about the **Mercedes Benz E-Class.** The rational values of the AMG E 63 S 4MATIC Sedan for instance, include amongst many others: Keyless Start, Tire Pressure Monitoring System, Back-Up Camera, Rain Sensing Wipers, Premium Sound System, WiFi, 8 Cylinder Engine, 603 Horsepower, Air Suspension, Automatic Parking etc.

The emotional values however, include amongst many others: a driving experience that reaches new heights, stylish and sporty exterior and interior, the highest level of ride comfort, driver assistance & safety, a new generation of infotainment, more efficiency etc.

Note that I got both rational and emotional values from Mercedes Benz websites (with some editing, of course).

An example most ladies can relate to is cosmetics. Let's talk about one of the products from my client - **Jules Organics Sparkle Oil.** The rational values of the product is amongst other things, high in unsaturated fatty acids, vitamins A, B1, B2 & B6, B complex, D and E and glycerol. It also contains over 12 organic oils, Evening Primrose, Calendula, Meadow Foam, Argan, Rosehip, Apricot Kernel, Macadamia, Sunflower, Castor, Sesame, Jojoba, Olive Extra Virgin Oil etc.

The emotional values include among others: a skin renewal regimen with organic components and vitamins, which are effective treatment for scars, dry skin, wrinkles, stretch marks dark spots, brown patches and acne. It also revives and rejuvenates the skin, leaving it soft textured and radiant.

Of course, you can tell which of the communication the customer is willing to pay attention to for their purchase decision.

Market research has proven over and again that emotional value is always the better foot to put forward when communicating with the customer. Truth is, people don't really care how many horsepowers or gigabytes that are packed in the product. Those rational values are important, no doubt, but they are not quite relevant to the person who wants to buy. They care more about what they perceive they desire in the product, how it makes them feel.

Customers make purchase decisions emotionally and then justify it with logic. This is not to discard rational value in your proposition to your customer. When you're pitching for the sale, focus more on saturating the customer with the emotional values and support your pitch with rational values.

I posted a video online sometime ago, featuring a movie scene where a lady was selling fabrics to a bride-to-be and her mother. In that video, I highlighted about 18 powerful selling techniques that you can deploy to make customer purchase decisions in your favour. Visit bit.ly/eniolasells to see the video.

More of these techniques are available at our trainings. Our online and offline trainings provide details on effective marketing communications and selling tips. If you'd like to be notified of future trainings or booking for private sessions for your business, kindly indicate in the review link at the end of the book, we'll keep you posted.

Oh, by the way, the winner at the episode of 'Invent It Rich' that I watched was a team that invented an automated ball launching device for dogs to fetch. This device was a fancy plastic hopper with a spout, that collects balls like tennis balls and automatically spews them out for dogs to fetch. Guess what the name of the product was? iFetch.

The product was targeted at customers with dogs who love to play fetch. The product is so user friendly that dogs could operate it by themselves by simply fetching the launched balls and feeding them back into the hopper. This was quite a selling point for customers who would love their pets to have an active lifestyle without necessarily walking them to the park or throwing balls for them to fetch all the time.

You can tell that this product scaled both the prototype testing and the consumer appraisal. The jury loved it and found it relevant to their everyday lives. What's more, the price point was friendly enough.

Success story, right there.

CHAPTER 5

HOW TO SELL AT YOUR OWN PRICE

"Some of the points in this chapter may not sit pretty with your orthodox business doctrine or school of thought."

Often times, business owners wonder if this is possible? To answer that question, I will be debunking a number of myths we have about the customer. This chapter is perhaps the longest in the book.

The previous chapters are deliberately kept short, so that you don't lose steam along the way and drop this book rather early. If you have made it this far, then you are indeed ready to deal with the real issues. Bravo!

Some of the points in this chapter may not sit pretty with your orthodox business doctrine or school of thought. I understand. It's okay. Don't be upset. You have a choice - consider the points you don't agree with as absolute rubbish, continue to do the same old things and expect a different result. Alternatively, you can give me a chance to prove myself by following my points of view to see if you'll actually get the different results you desire.

I believe that by the time we're done busting these ten customer myths, you will be able to stand on both feet and command the kingdom of your business, on your own terms.

TEN CUSTOMER MYTHS

1. Customer is king
2. Customer has limited budget
3. Customer knows what he wants
4. Customer of all types are yours
5. Customer is doing you a favour
6. Customer must not be sacked
7. Customer should be profitable
8. Customer runs your business
9. Customer is always correct
10. Customer must be loyal

1. CUSTOMER IS KING

Well, my question would be - "king of which kingdom?". Definitely not over the kingdom of your business, I presume. When two kings meet, you see a clear demonstration of mutual respect as they interact. Depending on which king is hosting the other, there is always a cordial atmosphere where the guest is not lord over the host, neither is the host lord over the guest.

The customer deserves some respect, no doubt. However, as a business owner or value provider, you must also understand your identity and your role - that you are a king, over the kingdom of your business. The concept of sales is that of value exchange. The customer wants something you have, you also want something the customer has.

Price is what the customer pays, while value is what you give. The customer is rarely subservient to receive the value he/she pays for. In the same vein, I see no reason why you should consider being subservient to receive payment for the value you deliver to your customer. If you fully understand the value you provide according to the previous chapters of this book, you'll be conscious of the fact that the customer needs you as much as you need the customer. There should be a mutual respect as you exchange values.

This myth has led some business owners to be oblivious of their worth and the value of their offering. Small wonder these businesses sell themselves short, below their product or service value just because they 'are desperate to sell', thus they end up running their businesses at the mercy of customers (that are unstable anyway), running into losses and eventually causing their businesses to fail.

It gets worse when these business owners live in denial and strive to please the customer at all cost, thus they take on the mindset of activity over productivity, where they believe it's better to at least, sell something and have some cash in hand. Very soon, the so called customer these business owners are referring to as king will wonder away to take over new territories.

2. CUSTOMER HAS LIMITED BUDGET

On this note, I'll also ask a question - "which customer are we talking about here?". Depending on the class of value you're providing, you can immediately figure out the class of audience you're targeting. Check out which of the following analogy describes the profile of your business if you generate a revenue of $1,000,000?

You sell 1,000,000 items at the rate of $1
You sell 100,000 items at the rate of $10
You sell 10,000 items at the rate of $100
You sell 1,000 items at the rate of $1,000
You sell 100 items at the rate of $10,000
You sell 10 items at the rate of $100,000
You sell 1 item at the rate of $1,000,000

I'm sure you get the picture. There are more than one route to your sales destination. It is your job to figure out which route works best for you. Most clients will tell you by default that 'they don't have money' or 'their budget is tight', but what they actually mean to tell you is that they don't want to pay more than the value they perceive they are getting from you.

When was the last time you went to the market as a customer and announced that you had enough money to pay whatever price the seller offered? Even Jeff Bezos or Aliko Dangote wouldn't do that. Whether a customer buys an item worth $1 or $1 million, he or she will always tell you he or she doesn't have money. It is your job to prove to the customer that he or she is getting the most value for his/her money - bang for the buck.

Let me also drop this here. Some business owners believe that the customer likes it cheap, but the reality is the customer likes a bargain or a deal. The term 'cheap' is often associated with a compromise in quality and value. Downward price review should be the last thing you consider after trying other options to secure the sale. Whenever your customer brings up price as the issue, there are a number of things you can do to give him or her a good feeling and a purchase decision in your favour.

First of all, defend your value offering by communicating it effectively to your customer in case you haven't done enough justice in that regard already. *If your customers don't understand or appreciate your value, they will not appreciate your discount.* **Never sell yourself short, else you lose your customer's respect.** Next, you throw in a few valuable bonus (accessories, shopping vouchers, free delivery etc) as an incentive to make the customer 'feel good' while buying. Also consider up-selling and cross-selling while you're at it, to give the customer the impression of getting more for less.

If you still find yourself struggling after applying these tips, you have two more things to do. Assess the customer, if he or she is really a prospect (who is truly interested in your value) or a suspect (who is just messing with you). I'm afraid, I can't teach you how to make that assessment. It's a bit of intuition and analysis of body language and chemistry that you have to figure out. If the customer is a prospect, you can look at your books and cut him or her a discount you're comfortable with. If the customer is a suspect, simply stick to your position on the transaction and let him or her figure out their exit. Remember, 'a Junkie finds the Means for a Fix'.

3. CUSTOMER KNOWS WHAT HE WANTS

This assertion is agreeable, but to an extent. It takes two to tango. As much as the customer knows what he or she wants, you as the business owner should know what value you provide. The customer may deny it, but the fact remains that he needs you to firm up the knowledge of what he wants. Let me illustrate with this personal story.

Sometime ago, I scheduled an appointment with my photographer for a portrait session. Before I got to his studio, he had sent me a message that he was running a little late, however, he had made arrangements with his associate to commence the photo session, that he'd join us shortly.

As a creative person, I had done a bit of research and saved quite a number of creative portraits I found interesting, to inspire the shots I'd have for myself. To a large extent, I knew what I wanted.

When we started the session, things were going on okay, as I was directing the shots. Before long, I was getting frustrated as the associate photographer was barely offering any creative input. He was simply pointing and shooting. I was the one correcting him about the position of the lights, the glare on my glasses, my shirt cuffs not sticking out of my jacket etc.

Shortly afterwards, the lead photographer joined us to see how things were going. I didn't spare a breath to vent my frustration. What he said in response shocked me. He said he had briefed his associate that I am an advertising guru, that I'd provide the creative direction of what I wanted, so he didn't have to worry. Immediately, I debunked the idea of him ceding the creative latitude to me alone, rather I wanted a robust session of collaborative ideas.

If Steve Jobs waited on the customer's knowledge alone, there would be no range of revolutionary Apple products. Henry Ford said in his famous quote that if he had asked what the customers wanted back in the days, they would have asked for faster horses.

This is a call to value providers to rise up and take their place in shaping customers desires with revolutionary solutions.

4. CUSTOMER OF ALL TYPES ARE YOURS

Here's to the hungry ones, the zealous value providers and the be-all-things-to-all-men types. If you continue in this line of thought, you might be sorry. One of the things you must understand is market segmentation. As much as I promise not to use technical jargon in this book, allow me to spell two things out here as simple as I can. Number one, **there are different kinds of customers.** Number two, **you are not sent** *to all of them.* There are customers meant for you and customers you are meant for. When you find each other, you will be fulfilled in your business.

Imagine trying to separate pebbles from fine sand. If you use three sieves of different mesh sizes, you will end up with three different sizes of pebbles and sand. Same applies to different types of customers. The different sieves refer to different business owners and value providers. The bigger sieves will sort out bigger stones while the tinier or fine-meshed sieves will sort out the fine sand. The stones you sort out are the ones you are meant to serve. Some customers will appreciate your business, others would not. Don't force yourself on the latter.

Every business is classified according to their class or position. Every customer is also classified according to their class or position. To attract the customers your business is built to serve, you need to position your business to align with the position of your customer. Whenever there is a positioning mismatch, there will always be a struggle with sales.

It's very easy to figure out which of your customers your business is built to serve. Simply go through your existing customers one-by-one. Evaluate how much it costs you to service each customer (phone calls, meetings, travels, man hours, deliveries, customer care, crisis management etc) and compare with how much you are earning in return for your efforts from the customer.

The goal is to sort your customers and prioritize them according to those who cost you the least to service and earn you the most value. For those that cost you much to service, but are still earning you good returns though, you need to manage them efficiently by finding creative ways to reduce your costs of servicing them while you increase your returns from them.

For the customers that are costing you more than you are getting in returns from them, I suggest you treat them as you see fit. Some of them might be worth a bit of investment for a little while before they start earning you more returns on your investment. Others might just be a waste of your time. Apply your intuition and analysis of their body language to decide if they're meant for you or not.

There would be times that business may be slow and you'd be tempted to fill the space with unworthy customers, just to keep busy. I beseech you, don't give in to that temptation. They will fill up that space in no time and drain you, yet they will not give you room to attract your ideal customers.

5. CUSTOMER IS DOING YOU A FAVOUR

Seriously? And you believed that? You must know by now that the feeling is mutual between you and the customer. From the myths we've busted so far, you understand better now that you seat on the same level as your customer and whatever you exchange as value is both agreed to be commensurate. In other words, you are both doing each other a favour.

Remember when we talked about trade by barter in Chapter 3, we established the fact that trading parties exchanged whatever they had for whatever they perceived as value from one another. Same principle applies today. The area many businesses consider a bit of concern is the competition threat by customers - the fear that the customer will walk away someday and take his business elsewhere.

Competition is really not a problem, if you look at it the right way. Competition is an inevitable motivation in business. It is your responsibility to be ahead of your competition. Again, I will squeeze in another technical jargon here, forgive me, I'll explain. Every business should have what is referred to as a Unique Selling Proposition (USP). This is simply referred to as your signature, that your customers cannot find anywhere else. Even if you and your competition offer similar value in the market place, the customer experience will definitely be different.

In the midst of competition, you must make the brand of your business irresistible and irreplaceable to your customer. Yes, I said it - brand. Does your business have a brand? It is imperative that you *build the brand of your business,* so that you can *reap the business of your brand.* I hope you understand that there is more to your brand than your logo and colours? Your brand is your overall identity, USP and every other thing that differentiates you from competition.

Strong brands don't worry about competition, they focus more on customer satisfaction. Think Amazon, Apple, Virgin, Tesla etc. Building the brand of your business is not an option, it is the life of your business. Details about brand building are covered in our trainings. Simply indicate at the readers review link (at the end of this book) if you'd like to be notified about new materials and upcoming trainings for your business development.

To understand the concept of focusing more on your customer and not your competition, I'll illustrate with a very interesting sport - Horse racing. When the horses are kept in their slots before the race starts, each horse wears what is called a pair of blinkers. These blinkers, also referred to as blinders are like sunglasses made from leather or plastic, attached to the horse's bridle to cover their eyes. The sides of the leather patch are blocked, so the only peep hole is in front. The whole idea is to prevent the horse from seeing what is happening beside it and focus on racing forward.

To each horse, the goal is the finish line, not the other race horses on the track. The horse is well groomed, trained and prepared for the race. Same for you as the value provider, your goal is customer super satisfaction, being irresistible and irreplaceable to the customer, not the fellow competition in the market place. Your business is well branded, your team is well trained and the value you provide is well communicated. Go ahead and run you race, focusing on customer super satisfaction and not the competition.

God speed.

6. CUSTOMER MUST NOT BE SACKED

Be advised that not every customer must be retained. On the flip side, it will be ridiculous to sack every customer. As a value provider, it is your responsibility to figure out which ones to sack and which ones to retain. Customers are an integral part of your business, they are a reflection of how your business is doing. Having at the back of your mind that all customers are not the same, it is your responsibility to do a routine audit of your customers to check if they align with your business goals. Just like germs and other unhealthy elements that do no align with your health goals find their way out of your system through pimples and boils, you need to creatively flush out unhealthy customers. Not all of them are for keeps.

Some customers are useful for some certain periods and you should appreciate their contribution to your business while it lasts. The moment they cease to add to you, you must understand that their job is done and it's time to move on, no sentiments. Just like you didn't hold on to those beautiful shoes when they wouldn't fit anymore, you let them go so you could get new and better shoes that fit.

Another interesting analogy is a river of fresh water. It is always available for use whenever you need it. However, the moment you try to create a dam to retain the water flow, after a while it begins to stink. If you don't let go of the stinking water, fresh water will not flow in.

It is your responsibility to hire and fire your customers. You have a business to run. You are not being arrogant, you are simply being true to your business. Your business is organic, it needs to grow. Just like a tree needs to be pruned for the branches to grow better and produce well nourished fruits, your business also needs to be pruned regularly for better growth. You need to audit each customer and decide if they are worth retaining, or like the boil on your skin, they should be relieved of duty.

I heard it somewhere that there are no permanent friends, nor permanent enemies, only permanent interests. Nothing stops customers you've fired from coming back, if they now have something to contribute to your business. That's why it is important that you manage your relationships carefully. Make peace with all men. Rather than burn the bridges, you can put a gate there for future access, if need be.

No sentiments. Eyes on the ball.

7. CUSTOMER SHOULD BE PROFITABLE

When I started my business a while ago, my mindset was 'Get Rich or Get Out!'. Well, I still hold on to the get rich part, but I have learnt a number of things along the way that made me review the 'get out' part.

We were taught, according to Pareto principle that 20% of our customers are bringing in 80% of our income, right? We were also taught that to build an effective crop of profitable customers, we should move the profitable 20% to the upper deck and kick the remaining 80% out of the ship to make room. Boy, our teachers were mean!

Fair enough, I applied this teaching in my business. At first, I felt really good that I had freed up space and was expecting more of the 20% profitable type of customers to flood in and fill my 80% void. Soon I realized something strange. Not only was I limited to my 20% profitable crop I had for a long time, even the little I had, started separating into two categories - one out of every five was being more profitable while the other four were dragging behind.

As accurate as the Pareto principle was, I didn't realize that it applies to whatever you have, even if you had taken from it. So, throwing the 80% customers overboard outrightly was not the solution. In hindsight, I admit that there's potential in the 80% I had discarded. I later realized that there is a process to managing your customer base, according to their profitability. Some of that 80% were actually profitable, if only I had worked on them.

Now profitability as defined in business is measured by how much is left after you deduct your product & service costs from whatever the customer pays in return. But for most businesses, financial profit is not all there is to the customer's worth.

Customer contribution is not only measured by its profitability. Some customers could be bringing in good income, coupled with so much stress. Some customers could be bringing in low income, coupled with huge profitable referrals. Some customers could be bringing in valuable feedback that inspire you to create revolutionary solutions. So you see it's not just black and white, look carefully through the spectrum.

8. CUSTOMER RUNS YOUR BUSINESS

That's not true. You run your business, not your customer, not even all of them combined. You created your business in the first place, not them. Remember, you're the king of the kingdom of your business. You own the vision that you set for your business, so why would you let anyone else run a vision they know nothing about?

The ongoing narrative is that we have promoted the roles that the customer plays in our businesses so much that we fail to see the role that we play in their lives as value providers. We have gone as far as saying that the customer pays the bills, the customer calls the shots, in fact, that the customer is god. This narrative is in itself, a myth.

The customer pays for the value you deliver and that's it. This payment is a bit of mathematics. The price you place on your product or service is the sum total of a number of things:
- Total cost of getting the product or service (raw materials, production, operations, processes, talents, concepts, consumables etc)
- Total cost of delivering value to the customer (packaging, marketing, transportation, logistics, customer care etc)
- Total overhead expenses and administrative costs
- Mark up percentage (profit as you see fit)

If you analyze the price indices, you'd realize that each individual customer in your portfolio is a piece in the whole puzzle. Even if you merge all your customers together, they are paying you for the value you gave them in return. In other wards, you are not in their debt, as long as the transactions are successful. Do not escalate the relationship to yielding control of your business to the customer.

Everybody loves control, even the customer. The more you exercise your control over your business, the more respect you earn from your customer. If you cede control of your business to your customer, you are in trouble.

9. CUSTOMER IS ALWAYS CORRECT

That is their opinion, not yours. Don't get me wrong. This chapter is not intended to antagonize the customer, but to set the records straight and have a balanced business relationship. If your mindset of the customer is flawed, your relationship with them will equally be flawed. This chapter is intended to prepare you to understand the customer better, understand yourself better and transact your businesses better without any sense of value exchange imbalance.

Both the customer and the value provider are humans. Perception, like I said earlier doesn't need to be accurate or factual, as long as the mind receives and processes the information available to it. Now the source of information available for the mind to process is a different kettle of fish altogether. There is a high possibility for both the customer and the value provider to have different opinions about a matter and yet be correct about the same matter in their own rights.

I believe what needs to be addressed here is not the correctness of the customer or the value provider, but the effectiveness of communication between both parties. As long as the mindset is sustained that one is correct and the other is wrong, what you'll end up with is an unproductive argument or a misunderstanding, which strains relationships.

To address the effective communication required in this case, I'll use a personal example.

Some time ago, my company designed a series of product packaging materials for a client. As a design company, we always recommend that our clients allow us to produce whatever concepts we design for them, to ensure a seamless operation and better still ensure quality consistency from concept to finish. Nonetheless, we communicate clearly with our clients that we respect their rights to produce wherever they wish.

After series of back-and-forth revision of the designs, the client requested for the artwork in production-ready format. They said they wanted to pass the artwork to their quality control department to proofread the details. We tried explaining to the client contact who made the request that they did not need a production-ready format file for proofreading, because the file would not be editable. The client contact couldn't see reasons with us and perceived that we were unwilling to grant their request.

The CEO picked up the phone and rang my number, asking why we didn't give them the production-ready file. He barely waited for my explanation when he raised his voice in an unfriendly tone, demanding immediate release of the file and hung up on me.

Did the client feel we withheld their file unnecessarily? - *Yes*.
Did I feel disrespected by the CEO's phone call? - *Yes*.
Did the client believe he was correct? - *Yes*.
Did I believe he was wrong? - *Yes*.

How did I react, knowing that a client has just disrespected me?

I remembered what my former boss used to say - "give the client what he wants, then give him what he needs". So I asked for the file in the requested format and emailed it to them, without any debate. Then I took some time off, to work on other projects that would help me calm down from the rage already brewing up in me (which is what I do whenever I feel that way).

When I was relaxed, I sent an email to the client (excerpts below, edited to protect relevant identities).

> *"If you need your Quality Control department to review and edit your packs, it is our job to advise you on the best file format suitable for such purpose. Production-ready format isn't what you need at such point, because the elements would not even be in open editable fonts anyway. A Hires open PDF format is best suitable for the purpose of highlighting and commenting for editing purpose.*

If however you wish to send the file for production and you simply let us know, we'd be happy to send you the final artwork without hesitation, prepared in Production-ready format because that is what is suitable for such purpose. We respect your right to produce wherever you choose, we only ask that you help us to help you achieve your goals.

Kindly be advised that sending you the final artwork (as we've done) implies that the design project is signed off satisfactory by you and completed by us. Any subsequent design requirement from our end on the same project would be considered additional work, which would attract a surcharge.

We believe we can have a wonderful working relationship, filled with mutual respect, mutual exchange of values and free of tension and unfriendly gestures.

Let us know if you need clarification at any point.
Thank you and regards."

Weeks later, I got a call from the CEO, asking for a favour about something else and the tone of voice was unusually respectful. I didn't get an apology (I wasn't expecting any), but we had a gentleman's conversation. That was the last time we had such situation.

From the email, you'll realize that I didn't confirm or deny that the customer is correct. I simply explained our work process to the client and inform them clearly of the consequences of their choices and actions. I also pointed out that our relationship is mutual and no party has any right to lord over the other.

I say it again. You are the king of your kingdom. If other kings have issues with your ways, simply communicate effectively with them and find means for mutual understanding. A difference in opinion doesn't always mean one party must take the fall.

10. CUSTOMER MUST BE LOYAL

Let me be frank with you. Customer loyalty is fickle. There's no such thing as customer loyalty. It is every Marketing professional's reality distortion field.

Why would I say such a thing? If we analyze the concept of loyalty, it speaks to a fidelity that is so strong. An adhesive force between two elements, difficult to pull apart. Loyalty is like an unconditional devotion to someone or something. It may take some time to forge, but it is very difficult to dissolve.

Customer loyalty however is like holding two pieces of wood with a paper glue. It may hold, but not for long. Customer loyalty is simply friendship with benefits. As a value provider, you must understand that customers will stick with you as long as there is something in it for them. That's why you need to be careful with your Giveaway Promos and Flash Sales.

I have seen instances where one of my clients was running Flash Sales almost back to back, because she felt that was when she was getting her customers' attention. Her business was bleeding in loses while her customers stuck to her like leeches. After a while, she thought she had gained customer loyalty and she justified her promotions with this mindset. When she couldn't sustain the Flash Sales anymore, her 'loyal' customers simply walked away.

Everybody is selfish, including you, including me! Let's not kid ourselves. Customers want the best deals and they could be promiscuous, if that's what it takes. We are all guilty. Deals are like drugs. If you don't use them properly according to prescriptions, addiction and abuse is inevitable.

I remember an online hub that trended in Nigeria a few years ago, specializing in offering the best deals in town. It started pretty nice, partnering with vendors that offered discounts from 40% - 70% off on their merchandise, then it spread like wild fire, hooking customers up like opium. At first, the deals were quite mouth watering, as the vendor partners were willing to use the platform to attract customers.

After some years, customers became junkies and wanted more. They shunned regular stores and looked forward to the Deals-of-the-Day from the hub. When the vendors could not sustain the discounts anymore, they started inflating the cost prices, thereby giving the impression that they were still offering discounts. The vendors forgot that their customers may be deal junkies, but they are not dumb.

When customers realized that the featured deals were really not deals when compared with regular stores, their loyalty was tested. Of course, they failed the test. Customers abandoned ship and the online hub started making a downward spiral. All of a sudden, the public realized without any formal notice that the online hub was no longer operational. It died, looking for customer loyalty.

As a value provider, I recommend you focus more on building your brand and satisfying your customers with your unique, irresistible and irreplaceable experience. Establish emotional relationships with your customers beyond business transactions. Have in mind that the customer will continue to make purchases everyday, so don't be too desperate to attract and retain them, just keep doing what you do best and your customers (who are already watching your consistency) will stay true to you.

CONCLUSION

In summary, we have focused on three key elements in this bundle - *value provider*, *value* itself and the **customer**. You now have the password into the mind of your customer and a manifest list of the value you carry. Your understanding of these elements and how they work together is your license to boosting your selling value.

I hope this book has been valuable to you, just like it has been to many other value providers and customers out there. Learning is the easy part and talk is cheap. The difference between you and the thousands that are going through this book is what you're going to do next with the information you have, starting with the next one week once you drop this book.

You need to set clear action points and delivery timelines for the three key elements discussed.
- **As a value provider**, outline your next steps to building the brand of your business. This will help you stand out from the competition and define how your customers perceive you. To achieve this, you need to:
  - Establish your unique selling proposition USP
  - Create your irresistible and irreplaceable signature experience etc.

- **For the value that you provide**, outline your next steps in investigating beyond the surface. This will help you understand and leverage on why your customers buy. To achieve this, you need to:
  * Find out how it makes your customer feel
  * Find out what desire it is satisfying.

- **About your customer**, outline your next steps towards understanding them better. This will help make your sales and marketing efforts more effective and reduce the shots you take in the dark. To achieve this, you need to:
  * Target them more accurately
  * Audit them periodically

If you have any challenge, or need help in carrying out any of these tasks as outlined, do not worry. I can recommend a competent and capable support to you. My company (Dafix Company) designs and promotes future-forward brands, brand identities and branding solutions for businesses. We can also provide advisory and consulting, to guide you to achieving your desired goals. As an owner of this book, we'd be happy to help you on your journey to delivering your next steps with readers discounts on our services. Simply send an email to dafixcompany@gmail.com and request a meeting.

Don't be a victim of analysis paralysis. You don't have to wait until you have everything figured out and all resources at your disposal before you launch. Things are better done than perfect. Start with what you have, where you are, then pick up more resources as you build your capacity.

We strongly recommend you look out for the remaining bundles in *The Selling Mindset* series and feed your mind with valuable content that is sure to improve your sales and develop your business.

A toast to your business success!

READER'S REVIEW

Thank you once again for making the smart decision to purchase this book. As we continually improve on our resources to serve you better, following sincere and valuable reviews we receive from readers like you, we would love you to spare a minute or two, to give us your review, in your own words. Simply visit bit.ly/readview. Thank you.

GET IN TOUCH

This is just the beginning. Let's keep the conversation going after this reading experience. If you'd like to have a chat with me on any part of this publication, or you'd like to be notified about future online / offline trainings, or interested in private sessions, or perhaps you'd love to join my online community for more extensive intellectual discourse, kindly reach me via dapoonamusi@gmail.com

Looking forward to connecting with you soon.
Sincerely yours,

Dapo Onamusi

ABOUT THE AUTHOR

Dapo Onamusi is unapologetically gifted in many ways. An engineer by training, he has unwrapped and polished his other colourful layers as a writer, ad man, coach, consultant, design thinker, drone pilot, speaker, salesman, photographer, videographer, graphic artist and then some. As a friend of God, Dapo is still work in progress...

OTHER BOOKS IN THE SERIES

THE SELLING ENERGY

ANYBODY CAN SELL. EVEN YOU!

THE ART OF GIVE AND TAKE

BUSINESS IQ VERSUS EQ

THE ATTITUDE CUSTOMERS LOVE

ACTIVATE THE 3Cs OF SELLING

www.ingramcontent.com/pod-product-compliance
Lightning Source LLC
Chambersburg PA
CBHW070244220526
45465CB00004B/1513